D0391262

First Year Student to First Year Success:

21 Things You Need To Know When Starting College

Hoping this a

great adventure —

♡

VL

2019

First Year Student to First Year Success:

21 Things You Need To Know When Starting College

Tom Krieglstein

Melissa Ruiz, MSW

Sabina Colleran

Illustrations/Design by Lia Rothschild

Editing by Jessi Ferguson

A Swift Kick Book

Copyright © 2016, 2018 by Swift Kick
All rights reserved. No part of this book may be reproduced in
any form without written permission from the publisher.

First Year Student to First Year Success:
21 Things You Need to Know When Starting College

Printed in the United States of America

Design by Lia Rothschild

REVISED EDITION (2018)
10 9 8 7 6 5 4 3 2 1

Swift Kick
www.SwiftKickHQ.com
sk@SwiftKickHQ.com
Phone: (877) 479-4385

>> Contact for bulk order discounts. <<

This book is dedicated to all students entering college
and starting a new chapter in their lives.

Table of Contents

Introduction 1

Section 1: Change 1, Change All 3

#1 Don't Panic; Plan it 5
#2 Veggie Chips and Tricep Dips 9
#3 Win the Morning, Win the Day 13

Section 2: #Adulting

#4 Spend Money... Wisely 17
#5 Make Money 20
#6 Save Money 23
#7 Mom? 26

Section 3: More Friends = More Fun

#8 Here's Your 7 Seconds 29
#9 Circle Up 32
#10 Humans Need Humans 35
#11 Proximity is Power 38
#12 Network = Net Worth 41

Section 4: Meh to Hmm

#13 Go Clubbing 45

#14 More to Your Core 48

#15 Feed Your Butterflies 51

#16 Raise the Tide 55

#17 Express Yourself 58

Section 5: Bring Your "A" Game

#18 Be Classy 63

#19 Get in the Zone 66

#20 Play to Win 69

#21 F(un-Stuck) 72

Conclusion

Go Forth and Be Awesome 76

Acknowledgements 77

About Tom 83

About Melissa 85

About Sabina 87

About Swift Kick 89

INTRODUCTION

After graduating high school with a "C" grade point average, I was rejected by almost every decent school to which I applied. I ended up enrolling at a college close to my childhood home that I knew would accept me, and I couldn't help but feel a sense of failure for not having gone to a brand name school. Like most first year students, I also felt excited, scared, and nervous about entering into a new chapter in my life. Despite a lot of uncertainty, the only thing I did know was that college wasn't going to be like anything I'd ever experienced before... and I was right.

My college had 34,000 students, which made it feel big, but most of the students commuted, which also made it feel small. The school devoted a massive amount of resources into helping me transition smoothly from high school to college. Yet after 90 days of hand-holding by the institution, I still had a backpack full of unanswered questions on how to succeed at this thing called college.

There was no rulebook for me to follow; no "12 Easy Steps to Mastering College." It was only through trial and error in my own experience, and learning from others' experiences, that I was able to eventually navigate higher education.

For the next three and a half years, I brought up my standing from "C" student to "Straight A " student. I even won a national academic award, graduated top of my class and got to deliver the commencement speech. It wasn't easy, but by figuring out some insider tips to college, I was able to excel.

Since graduating, I've worked with hundreds of thousands of students all around the world. A common phrase I keep hearing is, "If only someone would've told me [fill in the blank] when I started college."

The book you are holding is a combination of the super secret insider tips to college that either we, the authors, learned ourselves, or were suggested to us from our community of student leaders. This is the rulebook we wish we had when we were in your shoes. From classroom seating tips, to self-care techniques, to scoring the perfect campus job, this book is your insider's guide to college success that might not be covered at orientation.

You'll notice that the size, layout, and interactive sections of this book are all designed to make it your ultimate college field guide that you can squeeze into a backpack or coat pocket. Read straight through, or thumb to a topic that's most relevant to you. College can be one of the most exciting times in your life. With our field guide in hand, you're already well on your way to going from first-year student to first-year success!

- Tom

Change 1, Change All 3

Ever notice that when you get up from your chair and move around a little during a brainstorming session, you suddenly get a new idea? Or when you haven't eaten lunch yet and you start to get "hangry"? That's because the **three** parts of your state - your body, your emotions, and your mind - all affect one another. If you are feeling stuck, **change one** part of your state and **all three** will change.

TIPS

#1 Don't Panic; Plan it

#2 Veggie Chips and Tricep Dips

#3 Win the Morning, Win the Day

Tip #1
DON'T PANIC; PLAN IT

Growing up, keeping things in order was pretty simple: go to school, go to dance practice, do homework, go to bed, and repeat the next day. College, however, was a whole new ballgame. By my second semester, I was involved on campus in a lot more ways than just classes, and this made my schedule significantly busier.

To keep everything in order, I knew I needed a better system. One day, I was in the bookstore and saw the planner section and was taken aback by the wide array of choices. I picked the cheapest one (ballin' on a budget), went back to my room and started filling it in. Within two weeks, my planner was on me at all times. On a particularly busy day, I had scheduled back-to-back meetings with my team, followed by a one-on-one meeting with my advisor, two classes (one of which had a quiz), and a staff meeting for my on-campus job, followed by an event. Because I was still getting used to my planner, I mixed up the details of a few appointments. When I reviewed my schedule for the day, I noticed the issues, but had no room on the page to correct the mistakes. I told myself I would remember everything, but that didn't happen. From then on, I wrote only in pencil so I could make adjustments as needed.

My planner changed my life. It started off as a way to keep track of meetings, but then it became a place to scribble down ideas, keep track of homework assignments, and manage other tasks. It helped me be mindful of how I prepared for things. I learned to block out prep and travel time for events, dress rehearsals, and trips. My family has a saying, "I am going to be late to my own funeral", which, for me, has become less and less true because of my planner.

-Melissa

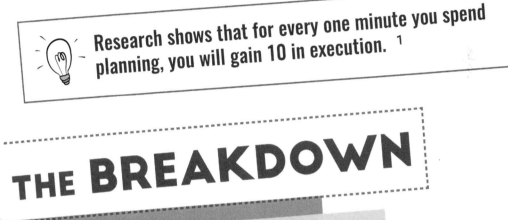

Research shows that for every one minute you spend planning, you will gain 10 in execution. [1]

THE **BREAKDOWN**

Half of the battle of getting everything done is planning the what, the how, the when. You cannot be successful in juggling the many different moving pieces of your life if you are only keeping track of everything in your head. Just the sheer act of remembering everything takes up all the space you need to do the tasks well. Find a good system that works for you and stick with it. Whether your weekly list is separated by class or by day, write everything down someplace you can always refer back to. There's power in knowing what your plan of attack is, and it gives you freedom to make decisions on what else to accomplish.

✓ DON'T MANAGE TIME, PRIORITIZE YOUR RESPONSIBILITIES.

The exam that counts for 50% of your grade is way more important than the paper that counts for 10%. If you're in a tough spot where you can't do both as well as you would like, prioritize the exam. You might want to work out, and go out with friends, and keep your A average, but some days you won't be able to do all three. Make sure you prioritize what's most important to you.

✓ PLAN FOR THE WEEK ON SUNDAY.

Before the chaos of a new week starts up, sit down with your syllabi and calendar. Jot down what you have due for the week, or in the coming weeks, that needs your attention. Take into account any events or commitments you have and figure out when the best time is to do each task, and work on actually following that schedule. The rest of your week won't be full of wondering what to do next, as you will have your plan ready to go.

✓ PLAN "YOU" TIME.

Do not let your planning become over-planning. Don't let a week become so full that you have no time to just sit down, or do something you enjoy. Remember that you will burn out if you don't plan time to unwind- all the planning in the world can't help you after that. You are allowed and encouraged to plan when you are going to have fun!

"I love deadlines, I love the whooshing sound they make as they fly by."

- Douglas Adams

YOUR CHALLENGE IS:

You have **168** hours in a week. Let's see how much time you spend on different parts of your life:

[ ] Eating

[ ] Sleeping

[ ] In Class

[ ] At Work

[ ] Hanging Out

[ ] Studying

+ [ ] Working Out

= [ ] Total

If you get a negative number, you might want to re-assess how you're spending your time!

Total

168 – [ ] = [ ] Time Left

In reflecting on how you spend the hours of your week, what is most surprising to you?

[ ]

Tip #2

VEGGIE CHIPS AND TRICEP DIPS

I admit it. I am guilty of staying up all night to write a paper.

It was my first semester and I had not yet started using my trusty planner. In high school, I had no problem writing papers at the last minute and getting a good grade. I thought it would be the same in college. NOPE. It was especially difficult when the topic in my Expository Writing class was globalization, something I had not yet mastered. Luckily, I had the other pieces of my life together.

I considered myself healthy and physically fit, as I was dancing in the on-campus dance club (think dance team, but not competitive) and exercising regularly. My diet wasn't as nutritious as it could have been, but because I was so active, I managed to avoid the dreaded "Freshman 15." A marathon study session would be no problem, I thought.

" One night of no sleep really took a toll on my body... "

When it came to this all-nighter, though, it took me the *rest of the week* to get back on schedule. One night of no sleep really took a toll on my body: my skin was dry, I couldn't focus the rest of the day and I napped every day the remainder of that week, thinking that would help. From then on, I set up a plan to break up assignments into smaller pieces and set up appointments with a tutor to make sure I was accountable for all my work. I did not want to re-live those seven days of exhaustion caused by my poor planning.

-Melissa

THE **BREAKDOWN**

> "A buffet for every meal in the dining hall? Yes, please."

> "The gym is on the other side of campus? Welp, that's never going to happen."

Sound familiar?

A buffet for every meal in the dining hall may seem like an awesome idea. But, without doing some push-ups and squats to offset that delicious omelette with all the fixings, it will end up looking like an inner tube on your gut.

Nothing good ever happens after 2am...go home. Sleep. It's a powerful thing. It can help you remember things you've studied, solve a problem, and even keep you out of trouble when other people are causing a raucous.

Move! Watching movies every night and all weekend may seem like the college thing to do, but you'll feel better about yourself by going to the gym and being active. Join (or start!) a running club or workout accountability group. You may even meet your future partner through these efforts!

Download an app to track your steps, how well you sleep, and for workout tips. Three grilled cheese sandwiches, chicken wings, fried rice, ice cream, two Cokes, cereal and a milkshake to-go will not get you a six-pack. Did you know the dining hall has **salad**? And **fruit**? And **vegetables**? Throw a few on your plate at every meal. Your future self will thank you.

 During the first 3–4 months of college, students gain an average of 1.5–6.8 pounds [...][2]

YOUR CHALLENGE IS:

A) Take a picture of your meal
(Paste a pic, draw it, or just jot some notes here!)

1. How many colors do you see on your plate?

2. Check all that you have:

☐ Protein ☐ Veggie ☐ Fruit

☐ Grain ☐ Water ☐ Healthy Fats

3. Was it delicious?

◯ Yes! ☺ ◯ No... ☹

B) Have an app that tracks your steps? Your goal should be 7,000 to 10,000 steps. Track how many steps you take each day.

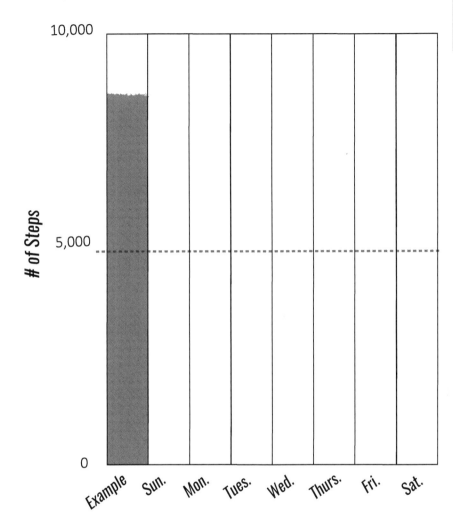

" YOU CAN'T EXERCISE YOUR WAY OUT OF A BAD DIET." - Mark Hyman

Tip #3

WIN THE MORNING
WIN THE DAY

After a long night of working and hanging with friends, getting up for my morning class was tough. Add in a 45 minute driving commute across the flat cornfields of Illinois, and I was in need of a desperate pick-me-up. At this point, most students would have reached for a cup of coffee, or two, but I was committed to figuring out how to wake myself up without getting addicted to caffeine. I found my alternative to caffeine in music. This wasn't just any music, but the same playlist of songs that I knew every morning would get me fired up and ready to take on the day. As soon as I got in my car, I cranked the volume and jammed away for the next 45 minutes. At red lights, the cars next to me couldn't help but stare and crack the occasional smile at the concert I was putting on in my car. By the time I got to school, the music had released enough endorphins in my body to keep me going until lunch time.

— Tom

"A daily ritual is a way of saying I'm voting for myself; I'm taking care of myself."

- Mariel Hemingway

Psychology Today discusses a survey of 68,000 people: 71 percent of bed makers consider themselves happy, while 62 percent of non-bed-makers admit to being unhappy.[3]

THE **BREAKDOWN**

Having a "Win the Morning, Win the Day " attitude is about knowing that tiny successes make for awesome days. A great way to do this is to make sure your day always starts with some positivity. Here are some ways to do this...

✦ **Make your bed every day.**

✦ **Recite positive affirmations.**

✦ **Make time for prayer or meditation.**

✦ **Write down something you are grateful for.**

✦ **Make exercise a daily morning habit- anything from yoga to weightlifting.**

✦ **Listen to music that will put you in a great mood.**

Add your own ways to start the day:

✦

✦

✦

✦

✦

YOUR CHALLENGE IS:

CHOOSE ONE of the ideas listed in The Breakdown and make it a habit for at least a week.

Which habit did you choose?

What changes did you notice in your overall mood after the week was over?

What surprised you the most by doing this new habit for a week?

#Adulting

College can be a rude awakening. Mom isn't waking you up anymore when you sleep past your alarm. You have to buy your own groceries and start thinking seriously about finances for the first time. Welcome to #Adulting.

TIPS

#4 Spend Money...Wisely

#5 Make Money

#6 Save Money

#7 Mom?

Tip #4
SPEND MONEY...WISELY

As I prepared for freshman orientation, I decided I wanted to look good and make an impression. I picked out a sundress, and instead of flats, boots, or any other comfortable shoe option, I went with heeled wedge shoes. As my father and I started the check-in process, I was feeling pretty good about myself, loving how my shoes pulled my outfit together, and thinking about how pulled together I must have looked to everyone else. That feeling soon changed, however, and sadly it was for the worse.

As the summer temperatures began to rise, I realized that the orientation day was to include a campus wide tour and my feet were already starting to hurt. Thankfully, my campus is set up in a circular format and there are only two hills. However, my tour group was unlucky enough to take the route that included both of those hills. Needless to say, by the end of the orientation, I was sweaty, miserable, and had three fresh blisters on my feet.

-Dakota

THE**BREAK**DOWN

You don't have to sacrifice comfort in order to look great. In thinking about your wardrobe, be sure to consider practicality in your selections.

We polled students and alumni in a private facebook group about what type of shoes are most important for a college student to have. 70% of the votes went to dress shoes.[4]

This new chapter of your life brings the need to buy things that you may have taken for granted while living at home. You might find yourself stuck wearing a hoodie on a rainy day because you never thought to buy an umbrella. The night before the career fair you may realize you have nothing professional to wear. It's important to be prepared for a variety of attire needs. Here are some tips:

Get good footwear: rain boots, comfortable shoes for walking, sneakers, dress shoes, flip flops for the shower

Make sure to have business casual clothing in case you want to go to a professional event.

Invest in an umbrella - you will thank yourself during your walk to class in April.

Are you at a school in a different climate than you grew up in? You might need a warmer coat for winter, or maybe more shorts for summer.

Section 2

It's inventory time! Check the items you have and make a note to do a little shopping for the rest.

- ☐ Rain Boots
- ☐ Umbrella
- ☐ Dress Shoes
- ☐ Athletic Shoes
- ☐ Comfy Shoes

- ☐ Appropriate Winter Outerwear
- ☐ Business Casual Outfit
- ☐ Dress-up Outfit for a Fancier Event
- ☐ Appropriate Warm-Weather Clothes

What other items would you consider necessary?

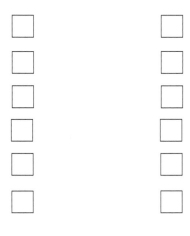

"Don't tell me where your priorities are. Show me where you spend your money and I'll tell you what they are."
- James W. Frick

Tip #5
MAKE MONEY

It didn't take long until I was known as "The Box Office Boy" on campus. My job was simple: I sat in a room, that was more like a shoebox, and sold discount tickets to the movies and occasional special events. On an average shift, I sold tickets to twenty students. With each transaction lasting only a few minutes, this gave me a lot of down time. Being in a room by myself, with an old-school computer that barely turned on, I didn't have many options but to do my homework. Over time, I started to solely dedicate the office hours to getting my homework done. The school didn't mind because they needed someone to staff their box office, and I didn't mind because I got paid to do my homework.

Prior to taking the role as "The Box Office Boy," I looked at other campus jobs in the printing center, academic advising, and the registrar's office. I learned quickly that not all student jobs on campus are equal in workload, but are equal in pay. With a little exploring and comparison, I landed the perfect campus job and will forever be known as "The Box Office Boy."

- Tom

Four out of five students are working their way through school, on average 19 hours per week.[5]

"People first, then money, then things."

- Suze Orman

THE BREAK DOWN

It's not so fun to be on campus with absolutely no spending money. But making some extra cash doesn't necessarily have to take away too much time from your studies or social life.

GET AN ON-CAMPUS JOB

Find a job that isn't too demanding so you can study while at work. Set work hours that work best with your class schedule and ability to get your homework done. Some examples: library clerk, tech support duty, staffing the box office.

A job will allow you to expand the work experience section of your resume during the school year.

SELL TEXTBOOKS WHEN YOU'RE FINISHED WITH THEM

Take care of them throughout the year so you can re-sell them in good condition.

Some venues to sell on: a textbook buy/sell group on social media for your campus; your campus bookstore; online e-commerce.

YOUR CHALLENGE IS:

Ask four different departments what type of student jobs they offer.
For each job, ask a current student in the role what the workload is like.

Job Title:

description:

Job Title:

description:

Job Title:

description:

Job Title:

description:

Tip #6
SAVE MONEY

My parents gifted me a large glass boot (a German tradition) that I converted into my own personal savings boot while in college. Whenever I came home with leftover change in my pocket, I would put it into my boot. At the time, a penny here or a quarter there really didn't matter. Over time, however, my savings boot filled up. By my sophomore year, my glass boot was overflowing with so much leftover change that I decided it was time to cash in. For fun, I had a few friends try and guess the total amount. We guessed between $50 and $100. Turns out we were all wrong...by a lot. The boot was holding just under $250 worth of coins! Such a small daily action of saving change turned into enough money for me to buy a plane ticket to visit my brother in San Francisco for spring break.

— Tom

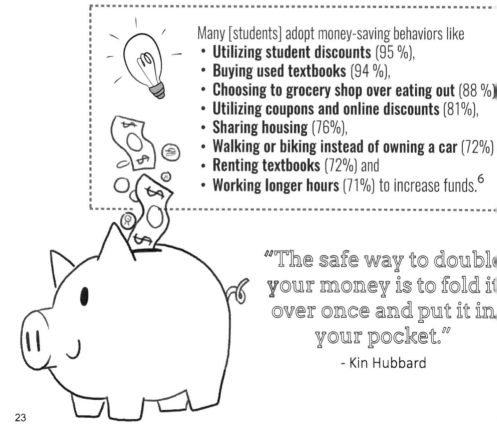

Many [students] adopt money-saving behaviors like
- **Utilizing student discounts** (95 %),
- **Buying used textbooks** (94 %),
- **Choosing to grocery shop over eating out** (88 %)
- **Utilizing coupons and online discounts** (81%),
- **Sharing housing** (76%),
- **Walking or biking instead of owning a car** (72%)
- **Renting textbooks** (72%) and
- **Working longer hours** (71%) to increase funds.[6]

"The safe way to double your money is to fold it over once and put it in your pocket."
- Kin Hubbard

THE **BREAKDOWN**

There are plenty of ways to be smart with your money while in college:

TEXTBOOKS (aka the biggest have-to expense)

Sometimes, it's worth waiting for the syllabus on the first day of class to see what books you need. Professors might change the required books from what was originally written on the bookstore website.

You **CAN** get your books cheaper:

- Ask your professor if an older or international version is okay.
- Browse sites that offer rental or used books.
- Buy from other students who used the book last semester.
- See if there's an eBook version.

EAT OUT ONLY FOR SPECIAL OCCASIONS. Money spent on food every day adds up really fast.

USE BIGGER PURCHASES AS INCENTIVES after a test or project, instead of buying impulsively. By that time, you'll be really sure you want it in the first place, and you'll be more motivated to study!

IF YOU'RE INTERESTED IN LEADERSHIP, see if you can apply to become a resident advisor or another position that pays for housing.

KEEP YOUR CHANGE. For example, when you break a $20, keep $2 for your piggy bank

PUT AWAY 10% OF YOUR PAYCHECK if you can. That way, every time you make money, you are building your savings account.

YOUR CHALLENGE IS:

For the next week, keep a spending journal. Write down what you bought and how much it was.

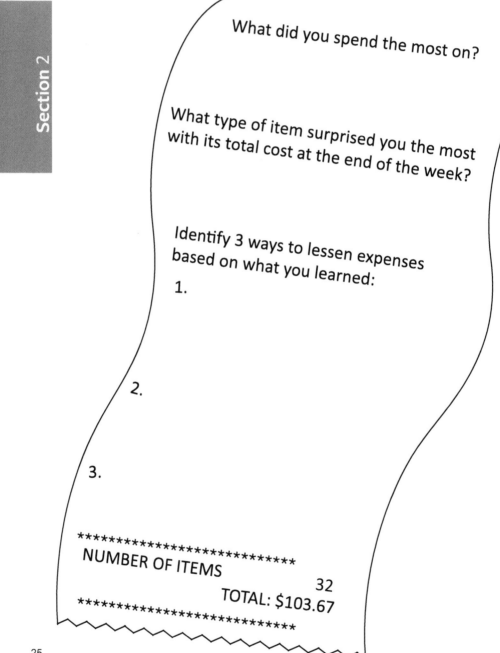

What did you spend the most on?

What type of item surprised you the most with its total cost at the end of the week?

Identify 3 ways to lessen expenses based on what you learned:

1.

2.

3.

```
***************************
NUMBER OF ITEMS
                          32
              TOTAL: $103.67
***************************
```

Tip #7
MOM?

 The median distance students go away for college is 94 miles. [7]

Growing up, my mom always told me to eat my greens, but what she neglected to tell me was how to cook them. While standing in the grocery store, I looked for the easiest, and cheapest, option to consume my daily greens, which led me to the frozen food aisle. For the next three months, my dinner after class consisted of some type of protein and a completely uninspired helping of frozen veggies, heated in the microwave. I didn't know about spices and seasonings or that fresh vegetables tasted better. It was my first attempt at being an adult, and on some level I succeeded, but on another level, I don't ever want to touch a frozen vegetable again.

– Tom

Section 2

THE **BREAKDOWN**

You are in charge of your life now. It's time for you to step up and no longer be a spectator. Your mom isn't going to pick up what you forget anymore. That's a good thing because you get to #adult now! :)

Make a laundry schedule and stick to it. Don't get stuck without underwear.

Find ways to learn accountability or get an accountability buddy to keep each other in check.

Be intentional about the groceries you buy. Look for healthy options and variety. Oh, and remember to go food shopping in the first place.

Take pride in staying on top of everyday tasks.

YOUR CHALLENGE IS:

Assign your tasks to days that work best with your schedule and pick an accountability buddy to check in with.

	Day of the Week	Accountability Buddy
Laundry		
Groceries		
Clean Your Space		
Exercise		
Call Home		

"...The independence of the mature person is simply that he does not collapse when he has to stand alone...."

-Nancy Chodorow

More *Friends* = More FUN

What makes any big transition **AWESOME** and easier? The people, of course. If you think about college like a dance floor, the more friends you have on a dance floor, the more fun that dance is going to be. It's simple- more friends equals more fun.

TIPS

#8 Here's Your 7 Seconds

#9 Circle Up

#10 Humans Need Humans

#11 Proximity is Power

#12 Network = Net Worth

Tip #8

HERE'S YOUR 7 SECONDS

On my first day of orientation, I met two students who would greatly shape those first few days, and the rest of my college career. For the sake of identity, we'll call them Jack and Joe.

Jack was the best kind of class clown. He made me laugh a lot and we were inseparable for what felt like forever. We were best friends and I told him everything. Joe was also a good friend, even though he came off a little more "too cool for school" to some. (I probably saw past that because I thought he was cute.)

Section 3

According to a Harvard study, it takes eight subsequent positive encounters to change a person's negative opinion of you.[7]

Fast forward a few months, and Jack totally burned me. He made several off-hand comments directed at me that weren't nice. A few months later, he ended up transferring to another school. Turns out, he was using college to be somebody he wasn't: a class clown to cover up his depression and past hurts. Joe, meanwhile, stayed by my side as a best friend all four years of college. We hung out, talked about life and careers, took classes together, served on the same board for our beloved club, and shaped each other's existence in many ways. Looking back, Joe is not someone I would normally become so close with, in terms of interests and personalities, but our circumstances threw us together and our friendship withstood the test of time. From the beginning, I would have thought Jack would be the one I'd be taking graduation pictures with, but in the end Joe was the one there snapping a selfie with me.

-Sabina

THE BREAKDOWN

It takes only seven seconds to make a first impression, which is why they are so important. When you initially meet someone, put your best self forward in order to connect. Be your authentic self and you'll attract the kind of friends you want to be around. Do not, like Jack, pretend to be someone you aren't, in hopes of fitting in. You'll attract the wrong people, and turn off the right ones.

When interacting with someone, it's important to trust what your instincts are telling you, but also find the balance to not judge a book by its cover. Had Sabina judged Joe by their initial interaction, they may not have ended up as such good friends.

"I don't know if you've ever noticed this, but first impressions are often entirely wrong...The first time you try Gorgonzola cheese you may find it too strong, but when you are older you may want to eat nothing but Gorgonzola cheese."

- Lemony Snicket

Find someone in your class you don't really know. Strike up a conversation with them. Afterward, reflect back here. What three traits or facts surprised you about that person?

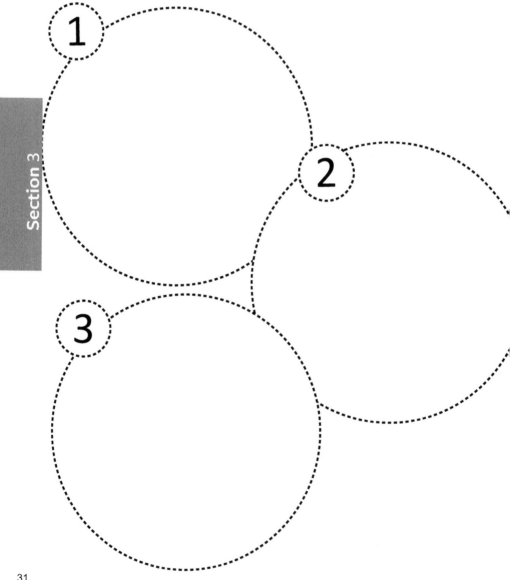

Tip #9
CIRCLE UP

When we started college, I was so excited to be roommates with Katie. While we weren't best friends, we had gone to high school together and I knew her well enough that the thought of living with her remained exciting. She was a biology major and her plan was to go to medical school. I was a psychology major and my plan was... still to be determined. At first, we did everything together. We checked out orientation events. We wandered the party scene on frat row. We went to the dining hall together and eventually connected with a group of girls I met during orientation that we both got along with.

Katie and I became busy enough with our own class schedules, meeting new people, and wandering the campus that when when it was just the two of us, we were totally fine to sit in silence, nap, eat, and be perfectly comfortable. When I was in college, there was an epic lineup of Tuesday night TV shows. Every week, we would pop some popcorn, leave the door open, and kick back. For two hours, Katie sat in her bed and I laid in mine as we binged on Tuesday night TV.

" Leaving our door open was a brilliant way to make new friends. "

At first, a few people we already knew would stop by and hang out. Then, as girls from the floor would walk by our door, they peeked in to see what we were watching. We welcomed each new girl into our room and introduced ourselves during the next commercial break. What started out as just familiar faces in the hallway, turned into a weekly "TV Night" tradition with a packed house, pillows, and popcorn. Leaving our door open was a brilliant way to make new friends. Our open door policy also helped Katie and me keep a positive roommate relationship because we had so many opportunities to meet and spend time with other people.

—Melissa

Section 3

> "I don't need a friend who changes when I change and who nods when I nod; my shadow does that much better."
>
> - Plutarch

THE BREAKDOWN

Just because you live with someone doesn't mean you have to be best friends. At bare minimum, you have to cohabitate in peace. Anything beyond that is a bonus. Your roommate should just be one of the many people in your group of friends, but don't let this group be filled with people just like you. It's a natural tendency to want to pair up with people who are similar to you because it's easy and safe. One of the greatest advantages of college is the network of diverse people you have the opportunity to connect with. Don't limit yourself. Build up a friend circle filled with diversity in ideas, experiences, and skills. It'll pay massive dividends for you later in life.

First-year college students who experience the highest level of exposure to different dimensions of diversity report the greatest gains in:

- **Thinking complexity (the ability to think about all parts and sides of an issue)**

- **Reflective thinking (the ability to think deeply)**

- **Critical thinking (the ability to think logically)** [8]

YOUR CHALLENGE IS:

List your 3 favorite traits about yourself.
Then pick 3 friends and write down your 2 favorite traits
about each of them that don't overlap with your own traits.

Me

....

Friends

1 name: ....

....

2 name: ....

....

3 name: ....

....

Tip #10
HUMANS NEED HUMANS

Every week, the resident advisor of our hall would try to get us girls to attend her "girls night" event. She would walk up and down the hall knocking on doors, yelling into bathrooms, and even cornering girls into agreeing to go. Week after week, I stealthily managed to avoid her and retreated to my room. My ninja skills met their match one night, however, as our RA could hear my roommate and me watching TV in our room and wouldn't stop knocking until we answered. After a long-winded conversation, we finally agreed to go to the event, as we figured that was the only way to get her to be quiet.

The first girls night I attended included twelve girls I didn't know, my roommate, and the RA. The night began with storytelling revolving around our most embarrassing dating experiences. The first girl to share was nervous as she told a dreadfully laughable story. I went next, knowing I had a story to match. Beyond our dating stories, I noticed several similarities between myself and the first girl throughout the night, so I eventually introduced myself. Years later, she's one of my best friends and she even asked me to be a bridesmaid in her wedding.

-Dakota

Hundreds of scientific studies over the past decade have shown that having at least two strong social relationships dramatically increases positive health outcomes and helps us succeed in our goals.[9]

"THE ONLY WAY TO HAVE

College is way more fun when you are experiencing the adventure with friends. New friends, however, don't just appear. You have to go out there and make it happen. Don't go home after your class; instead, sit on a bench in a common area. Be open to making connections to people around you.

Smile and say hi (not creepily) at people passing by. When you dig into a conversation with someone, be more interested in what they are saying than trying to make yourself more interesting. As the saying goes, you have two ears and one mouth, use them in proportion when trying to make friends.

A FRIEND IS TO BE ONE."

- Ralph Waldo Emerson

YOUR CHALLENGE IS:

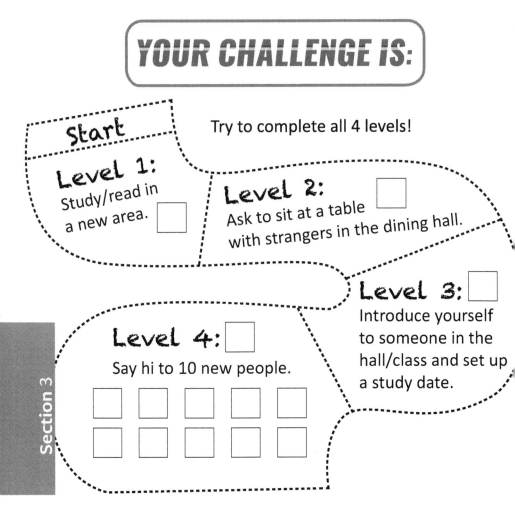

Try to complete all 4 levels!

Start

Level 1: Study/read in a new area. ☐

Level 2: Ask to sit at a table with strangers in the dining hall. ☐

Level 3: ☐ Introduce yourself to someone in the hall/class and set up a study date.

Level 4: ☐ Say hi to 10 new people.

☐ ☐ ☐ ☐ ☐
☐ ☐ ☐ ☐ ☐

Which level was your favorite?

1   2   3   4

Why?

Did you make lasting connections?

Yes   No

With whom?

Tip #11
PROXIMITY IS POWER

With the tiny amount of extra time I had left in my calendar, I opted to sign up for an Emerging Leaders course on campus. Besides the course description being interesting, the element that caught my eye the most was that the course was being co-taught by the Assistant Dean of Students, Dean Brown, and the Director for Student Activities, Anna. I had never heard of a class on campus being taught by an administrator before, so I jumped at the chance to sign up.

It didn't take long for Emerging Leaders to become my favorite class. Conversations in this class were honest and the stories from Dean Brown and Anna were off the charts! I didn't want to become a teacher's pet in class, but my pure excitement for the course propelled me to engage every chance I could. Even after class, I would stop by Anna's office to ask questions about assignments or to continue a class conversation. In turn, Anna and I got to know each other really well.

One day, I was walking with Anna back to her office and she mentioned there was a board meeting that evening for an annual event on campus, and she invited me to attend. I decided to go and within a week, I was the Public Relations Chair for the student group! From there, Anna continued to open up many doors for me. I was even nominated to give the end of year student leadership recognition speech, an honor that came about as a result of the time and energy I had dedicated to working with Anna and Student Activities.

-Melissa

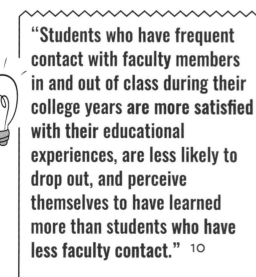

"Students who have frequent contact with faculty members in and out of class during their college years are more satisfied with their educational experiences, are less likely to drop out, and perceive themselves to have learned more than students who have less faculty contact." [10]

THE BREAK DOWN

Ever hear the phrase, "It's not what you know, it's *who* you know?" College isn't just about connecting with your fellow students; in fact, if you just connect with your peers, you are missing out on one of the greatest resources a college has to offer...its employees. Faculty, staff, and administration have an amazing ability to provide students with exciting opportunities. Make it a point to go out of your way to connect with the college personnel beyond casual greetings. Even a lunch lady or janitor might open up doors you never would've expected. Think about ways you can offer a helping hand. University employees are accustomed to hearing about the troubled side of the student body, so when you talk with them, be sure to share positive updates too. Getting them to smile and laugh with you will go a long way to building a connection.

"One repays a teacher badly if one always remains nothing but a pupil."

- Friedrich Nietzsche

YOUR CHALLENGE IS:

From the list of campus employees below, circle three. Then find each employee you chose on campus and introduce yourself. Find something in common with them, then take a selfie with that person and upload it to social media, using the tag #21TipsBook.

- **Professor**
- **Student Life Office Secretary**
- **Maintenance Staff**
- **Cashier in Cafeteria**
- **Security Guard**
- **Financial Service Staff**
- **Teaching Assistant**
- **Librarian**

Tip #12
NETWORK = NETWORTH

As I was finishing up my college career and looking forward to graduation, I had finally come up with a perfect system for getting all my homework and leadership duties done each week. I was pretty happy with it, so you can imagine my joy when a friend asked me for advice. She wanted to know my procedure, how I balanced everything, and kept myself on track. I gave her a detailed outline of my system, happy to pass along what had taken me three years to perfect.

I am willing to bet that she had a higher IQ than I did, but what made her even more intelligent was her willingness to ask for advice from an upperclassman. Since that day, we've swapped thoughts on original poetry, shared countless messages of support, and she's even written for my organization.

I saw her a couple years after graduation at an alumni event. Once again, I was struck by her success and insightful mind, as she spoke about her career at a respected financial institution. She may have been concerned that semester about her ability to follow a checklist, but it's safe to say she has excelled since.

- Sabina

THE BREAKDOWN

You are the average of the ten people you keep around you, so choose wisely. Your friends' attitudes will impact your attitude. Your friends' health will impact your health. Everything your friends do will reflect back on you in some way. Surround yourself with people who add to your life, not subtract. Look for the motivated students on campus and build a relationship with them. It's no secret that 'A' students hang around other 'A' students. If you are struggling in one area, ask your more successful friends for tips and spend more time with them. Together, the right group of friends can go a long way.

 Student's values, beliefs, and aspirations change in the direction of the dominant values, beliefs, and aspirations of other students.[11]

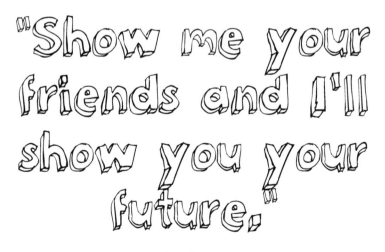

"Show me your friends and I'll show you your future."

- Lee Brown

YOUR CHALLENGE IS:

Write down the names of two people who you know that seem to be successful students. Ask them to describe their system for getting things done, and record them here.

name: ....

description:

name: ....

description:

What system makes more sense for you?

How could you incorporate their tips into your own life?

Meh to Hmm

"Meh" (*adj*): being uninterested and not engaged with the environment

"Hmmm" (*adj*): being curious and paying attention to the surroundings, in order to get involved

You're in charge of your own curiosity, excitement, and adventures. College is all about experiencing new ideas and opportunities. The choice is yours and will make all the difference to your current and future success, so get out there and push yourself to go from "Meh" to "Hmmm."

TIPS

#13 Go Clubbing

#14 More to your Core

#15 Feed Your Butterflies

#16 Raise the Tide

#17 Express Yourself

Tip #13
GO CLUBBING

During my freshman year, I attended a FUPAC (Fordham University Philippines American Club) meeting because my half-Filipino friend was running for a board position and I wanted to be there to support him. What I didn't know at the time was that from that point on, I would never stop going to FUPAC meetings each week. I had no idea that FUPAC would become the center of my universe at Fordham, my on-campus family, and my heart. I didn't know that I would run for Internal PR my junior year, and run for Vice President my senior year. I definitely didn't know that I would work harder and more passionately to make the FUPAC organization more successful than I had for anything else before.

> ❝ I never would have gotten any of that had I not decided to go to a meeting where some might think I didn't "belong." ❞

When I tell people I was VP of a Filipino club, they look at me funny and then ask if I am Filipino. I'm actually 100% Italian, but we used to joke that I was Filipino at heart. I learned so much about the culture and felt at home with the people in the club. I learned about being a leader and about who I was meant to be as a person while serving and participating in FUPAC. I never would have gotten any of that had I not decided to go to a meeting where some might think I didn't "belong." Even I thought that, at first. Had I never tried, I never would have known about this culture I was meant to explore. I could have decided FUPAC wasn't my scene and joined the Italian club, the school paper, or the photography club, but instead, I got extremely lucky and found my niche in the first few weeks of college. I never looked back.

- Sabina

> "I had no idea when I went to college what I'd be doing... I took many courses and participated in as many activities as I could. I learned a lot about every single thing."
>
> - Martha Stewart

THE**BREAKDOWN**

Go clubbing! No, we're not talking about that kind of clubbing, so put your shiny shirt and glow sticks away. We're talking about the importance of being involved in a student club or organization outside the classroom. A massive amount of research states how valuable it is for a student to not only be successful in class, but also have a well-rounded balance with extracurricular activities and service projects. In short, get involved on campus!

In a study at California State University-Sacramento, students involved in extra-curricular activities consistently achieved higher GPAs than those who were not involved on campus.[12]

The Student Activities office can give you more information on how to get involved on campus. Sign up for a few student club newsletters and see which ones you like the best. Test out a few groups by attending their next event. Be careful though- don't get too involved too quickly and overcommit yourself. Once you have a strong sense of which group(s) you enjoy the most, jump in and give them your best effort. You never know, you might land yourself a leadership position faster than you think.

Find a list of student organizations on your campus or go to a club fair. From that student organization list, identify:

A Current Interest: --

An Unexplored Interest: --

A Wild Card Option: --

Go to at least one meeting for each club you selected.

Tip #14
MORE TO YOUR CORE

I had a great academic advisor at my college. He helped me create schedules that "double (or triple!) dipped" with all the requirements for my degree. This meant that by my junior year, I was taking only four classes per semester. By senior year, I managed to take only three per semester and still be considered a full time student. My schedule was so efficient that I even had time to take classes just for fun. A psych major has no requirement to take "Effective Speaking", "Drawing," or "Visual Thinking." But goodness gracious, I took them, and I took them with fervor.

I ended up learning more in my "just for fun" Visual Thinking class than I did in any other class during my four years in college. Visual Thinking is an art class that focuses on different mediums (paint, wire, pencil, collage) and using them in ways that make a person re-think how they perceive their work. My final project was a magazine collage based on a painting I saw in a gallery that inspired me. I recreated the painting, and was amazed at what I had made. This class unlocked a potential in myself that I had no idea about. Who knew I could create a life-like nose out of different colored pieces of glossy paper? Who knew I could become so passionately involved with the process that I finally understood the notion of artists falling in love with their work? By taking a class to explore an interest and not a requirement, I found myself more invested in the actual learning. (You know, the whole point of college.)

My Visual Thinking class was one of the hardest classes I ever took, but it also was the most fulfilling. It taught me that I could successfully be an artist. It taught me to solve problems when the medium I was using didn't allow erasing. It taught me that "impossible" is only relevant until I try to make something beautiful.

- Sabina

When it comes to landing a job, an internship is far and away the most valuable extracurricular to have on your resume. According to 2010 Boston University survey and 2008 NACE survey, students who had an internship:

53% job offer by graduation

75% preferred in hiring[13]

31% higher salary

"YOU CAN LEARN NEW THINGS AT ANY TIME IN YOUR LIFE IF YOU'RE WILLING TO BE A BEGINNER. IF YOU ACTUALLY LEARN TO LIKE BEING A BEGINNER, THE WHOLE WORLD OPENS UP TO YOU."

- Barbara Sher

THE **BREAKDOWN**

Despite the fact that you get to select your own courses in college, the majority of your classes are going to be predetermined for you based on your major. Your schedule will fill up fast and before you know it, you'll be graduating. Don't let your schedule fill up with only required classes. If you can, make room for a few electives or an interesting internship. Open any college course catalog and you'll see topics ranging from speech to art to science fiction. Explore some of your fringe interests either in the classroom or with a company as an intern. College is the place to test the waters to learn about new ideas. If you are concerned with an elective class impacting your GPA, take a pass/fail option or find a one credit class just to get your feet wet in a fun topic.

Identify three of your interests that are offered as classes.

1 ....

2 ....

3 ....

List three dream internships you'd love to try.

1 ....

2 ....

3 ....

Talk to your advisor about how you can incorporate these into your college career.

Tip #15
FEED YOUR BUTTERFLIES

I started my college career proudly telling my student group that I was a follower, not a leader. I felt that my role was to support from the crowd, while someone else did the leading and organizing. Then, something changed at the end of my sophomore year and I found myself doing something I never would have expected. At the same time that I applied to be the Internal PR of my club, I also applied to be an orientation leader. I decided that if these things terrified me, then I needed to do them.

Both of these experiences turned me into the person I am today. I became a leader with big ideas, learned about serving those around me, and felt the adrenaline rush every time I put my natural talents to work. These are the experiences that got me my first job right out of college and taught me what it feels like to be passionate about a group of people and an institution. Years later, I look back on my memories at Fordham and still feel ridiculously grateful to have been a part of it all.

On the other hand, I had to learn when to say NO to opportunities. The year after serving as Internal PR, I ran for Vice President of the club and won the race. That same month, friends of mine from the Commuting Students Association asked me to join their team, too. I was flattered and genuinely considered it. In the end, I decided my heart was with the club I was already serving, and if I tried to do both, I couldn't give my all to either organization. My friends were upset but I had to stick to my decision. I had learned that I did my best work when I was focused on one project, not spread out. My year as Vice President was difficult, but it was also th most enjoyable stress I have ever experienced. I would do it again in a heartbeat.

- Sabina

30% of Americans continue to be fearful of things that happened in their past.[14]

"We are not going to live by our fears, we are going to live by our hopes." - Mike Tomlin

THE BREAK DOWN

College is a crazy, fun, whirlwind of experiences and emotional roller coasters...and that is part of what makes it great! It's okay to be overwhelmed; the true experience comes from how you react to it all and what lessons you learn. Take risks, step outside your comfort zone and learn to laugh at yourself.

On the flip side, many opportunities will be one decision away from a really fun time, or nothing but trouble, so know your limits. It's okay to say no to things and/or people that take you too far out of your realm of security. Only you can create those boundaries.

Join that club, go on that camping trip, talk to that cute person in class. No effort, no results!

Section 4

YOUR CHALLENGE IS:

Of the following activities, place them into the circle that most relates to the feeling it gives you:

- Sky diving
- Trip to amusement park with strangers
- Public speaking
- Joining a new club
- Staying in instead of partying
- Talking to the person you are interested in
- Asking a professor for help
- Taking a dance class
- Singing class
- Acting class
- Learning a new language
- Learning to drive
- Going to the movies alone
- Going to dinner alone

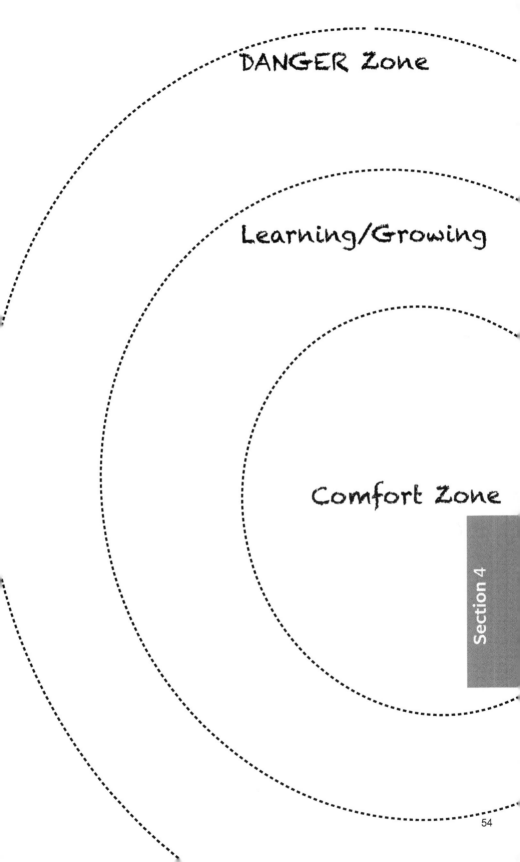

DANGER Zone

Learning/Growing

Comfort Zone

Tip #16
RAISE THE TIDE

"RJ meet Tom. Tom is your new big brother. Tom meet RJ. RJ is your new little brother." The agent from the mentorship organization smiled as she saw our hands shake and knew we were a perfect match. She was right; we instantly connected.

At 21 years old, I didn't exactly know what I was getting into, as this was the first time in my life that I was asked to be a mentor to someone else. Why would someone want to listen to me? What do I know that other people don't? As it turns out, being a mentor to someone else was exactly what I needed to help me reach my next level of success.

Most people think being of service to someone else is just about benefiting that person, but RJ gave so much to me by letting me be his big brother. He pushed me to be a better person because I wanted to be a better role model for him. As a result of his questioning, I relearned some of life's most basic lessons by teaching them to him.

— Tom

THE BREAKDOWN

How do you spend your free time? Watching TV? Taking a nap? Sure, that's college. But this section is about stepping it up a bit. Think about someone you look up to. How much time do you spend with them? What experiences do they have that you don't? Chances are, their experiences can help guide you on what to do next. Now, think about a friend or peer. How much time do you spend with them? What do you learn from them? They are probably the easiest to talk to, since they share your journey. Finally, think about someone with less experience than you who might look up to you. How much time do you spend with that person?

It may seem unrealistic, but in actuality, spending equal amounts of time with these different groups of people will give you the right balance of perspective, support, and action.

"The best way to find yourself is to lose yourself in the service of others."

- Gandhi

In 2015, volunteer rates among 20-24-year-olds were at 18.4%. Teenegers (16-19-year-olds) had a volunteer rate of 26.4%.[15]

YOUR CHALLENGE IS:

In reflecting on your current life, estimate the hours you are spending wit
mentors, peers, and volunteering.

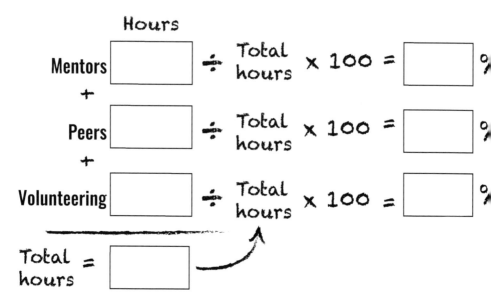

Hours

Mentors [ ] ÷ Total hours × 100 = [ ] %

+

Peers [ ] ÷ Total hours × 100 = [ ] %

+

Volunteering [ ] ÷ Total hours × 100 = [ ] %

Total = [ ]
hours

In the spaces below, write one action you can do to help better balance
the amount of time you are spending in each area.

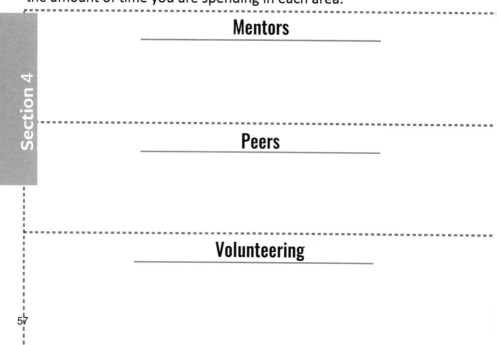

Mentors

_____

Peers

_____

Volunteering

_____

Tip #17
EXPRESS YOURSELF

"This is my first time writing in a journal. I got the idea from a speaker who came to my campus this afternoon. He said to just trust him that it'll be worth it. So here goes nothing."

I wrote those words towards the end of my first year in college. Since then, my journal has been a constant companion to the ups and downs of life; a friend who will listen to me without judgment.

One topic that repeatedly kept coming up in my journal throughout college was what I was going to do with my life. Here are three lines from the many entries I wrote on the topic:

"I'm so confused about what I should be doing with my life."

"Why is this so complicated to figure out?"

"Am I the only one? It seems like everyone else is so clear on their life path."

Each time I wrote down my feelings about my future, my anxiety level would decrease. Over time, my writings turned from anxiety and questions into clarity and focus. Journaling really did work for me.

Looking back, I can now see how valuable journaling has been for my development throughout college. The speaker I met my freshman year was right, journaling is totally worth it!

– Tom

The National Association of Colleges and Employers 2015 study found that 70.2% of surveyed employers look for written communication skills in new college graduates, and 68.9% were looking for verbal communication skills.[16]

THE **BREAKDOWN**

As you start to explore who you are and what you want to learn in college, new opportunities will come your way. A lot of these opportunities will allow you to gain experience in communicating effectively- a priceless skill to have. Use them all. Start with one or two and see where it takes you.

Section 4

Here are some ideas for becoming a better writer and speaker on your own time:

Start a journal to help solve a problem and be able to reminisce one day on your college experience.

Have an opinion about something happening on campus? Submit an op-ed to your college newspaper.

Take a public speaking class, especially if you know that presenting in front of people is not your strong suit.

"To speak and to speak well, are two things. A fool may talk, but a wise man speaks."

- Ben Jonson

Start a blog about a topic you are passionate about, and ask your friends and family for feedback.

Recognizing new opportunities to express yourself through language will help you not only when it comes to writing papers, but outside of the classroom when it's time to network.

YOUR CHALLENGE IS:

Start a journal!
Here are four prompts to help get you going:

Write about the best or worst day of your life.

Describe someone you consider a hero. Who is that person and why?

If you could go anywhere and "anywhen" in time, when and where would you go?

What is one thing that makes you the happiest? The saddest? The most scared? The most hopeful?

Bring Your "A" Game

Remember, you're in college for academics first. When you successfully make an effort to be awesome in class, you will have the time and motivation to be awesome in all aspects of your journey.

First and foremost, you should have clear goals about how you want to perform in your classes. Take steps early on to get there. College classes are very different from your high school experience. Professors probably won't remind you about a quiz coming up, or even that you have to read a certain section of the book. Taking the lead and independently creating and focusing on your academic goals will set you up for success.

TIPS

#18 Be Classy

#19 Get in the Zone

#20 Play To Win

#21 F(un-Stuck)

Tip #18

BE CLASSY

Studies show that students who sit in the front and center (middle) of the classroom tend to achieve higher average exam scores. [18]

Maybe it was cruel. Maybe it wasn't. Our marketing teacher loved to publicly post the results of each student's overall grade after each test. It wasn't by name, but rather by school ID. Despite the teacher's attempts to hide our identities, everyone in the class knew the top slot was often a battle between Sarah and myself. Sarah was naturally wicked smart and a hard worker. She consumed knowledge like I consumed food. Most would assume Sarah should easily own the top grade slot...if it wasn't for me. More often than not, I ended up beating Sarah for the highest score. As someone who graduated high school with a "C" grade point average, and often doesn't get asked back to trivia night, I can assure you I am not the connoisseur of knowledge that Sarah was. What I lacked in natural brain capacity, I made up for in mastering the tricks of the classroom. I leveraged the natural tendencies of the teacher to figure out how to trick my brain into remembering information, studying more efficiently, picking the right answer on tests, and ultimately getting the highest grade in the class.

– Tom

THE BREAKDOWN

We know, we know. Class...ugh! But if you go into academics with a "ready to learn and participate" attitude, you're going to gain a lot of value. That is what you're paying for, after all.

But, here's the thing: you can get a lot more out of class than just what's going to be on the next quiz or test.

Make friends in class, especially if they seem to have a solid grasp of the material. Find a few people and make a study group. Include someone that takes really good notes, someone that knows the material inside and out, and someone that asks really good questions. This combination will make for a productive study session.

Sitting next to distracting people is only going to...DISTRACT you! Sit near people who will motivate you to pay attention, not play on social media. It's the difference between being confused on the test and being amazing.

Heard of the T-zone? No, not the area on your face that every beauty company tells you about. This T-zone is in the classroom, and includes the front row and seats down the center of the room. This is the high traffic zone for a professor, as they typically walk back and forth or stand center at the front of the room. Sitting in this area will help you pay more attention, simply because you have more attention on you, especially in a small classroom.

Not a good test-taker? Here's a cool trick: If you're stuck on an answer, pick the one you can defend the best to the professor if you get it wrong. Maybe there is some partial credit in your future.

Visual learner? Doodle! Yes, studies have shown that doodling is a way to promote processing of information in the brain.[17] This is person specific, but give it a shot and see what happens.

Have notebooks full of pages in all the same color? When studying, go back in and add notes or acronyms with a different color pen. Those pieces will stand out in your mind, making the information a little easier to recall later.

These are just a few of the ninja classroom tips you can pick up as you take classes.

"Encouraging a focus on effort rather than raw intelligence or talents, helps make [students] into high achievers in school and in life."

- Carol S. Dweck

To get started on your study group, write down your hardest classes and get the name and contact info of 3 people in each class.

Class 1: ....

....

....

....

Class 2: ....

....

....

....

Class 3: ....

....

....

....

Class 4: ....

....

....

....

Sit in the **T-zone** for at least 5 class sessions:

✓ ☐ ☐ ☐ ☐ ☐

Tip #19
GET IN THE ZONE

"I Kant even!" That's what I used to say when studying the great philosopher Immanuel Kant. I remember being completely done with trying to read the dense texts, let alone understand them. But as a dedicated student, I tried to do my readings and assignments as best as I could. One afternoon, I was home with Kant, and my little sister was sitting in the room with me. I started reading Kant's work out loud with a British accent. (Or, my best attempt at a British accent.) Not only did my sister and I get lots of amusement from my silliness, but I did something right. You'll be just as surprised as I was to learn, years later, that my sister remembered some of the content from the Kant readings I was doing, because she remembered my accent.

- Sabina

On average, it takes {people} a whopping 23 minutes and 15 seconds to get back to their original task once they are interrupted.[19]

It always seems impossible until it's done.

- Nelson Mandela

THE **BREAKDOWN**

Now that you know how much time you have "left over" in a week (see tip #1), it's time to start focusing certain parts of your week on things like preparing for class and, wait for it...STUDYING! Set aside one day every week or a few days per week to study. **Don't cram once finals come around.** Not only will it be harder to remember all that information, it's just not worth the stress.

When you do get into those homework and study sessions, **try single tasking.** Set an alarm to study for 50 minutes, then take a 10 minute break to recharge before diving back into the work. This state change will give you some energy and allow your brain to process information. You can change the increments to best reflect your available time. For example, if you have 90 minutes and want to work on a project, set your timer for 40 minutes of work, a 10 minute break, and 40 more minutes of work.

Have you ever tried to teach a lesson to someone else and ended up understanding it a little better yourself at the end of it? This technique is very helpful in making sure you have a grasp on the information. Team up with a classmate and take turns teaching each other the material as a review of what you learned in class. **To teach is to learn.**

Try throwing in a funny accent when you're teaching. This silly exercise makes the information even more memorable. When you actively engage with the material, you learn more effectively.

Environment is everything. Do you like to study in silence or do you prefer a little background noise? Is a window helpful to your productivity? Do you like to wear the clothes you wore all day or study in your pajamas? Keep water and a snack nearby so you don't waste time or procrastinate when you get a little hungry or thirsty. Knowing how you best study helps you create the environment that best suits your needs.

YOUR CHALLENGE IS:

To teach is to learn. Write down how you would explain the lesson from your last class to a 5 year old.

Tip #20
PLAY TO WIN

As soon as the teacher dismissed the class, everyone would bolt towards the building exit as fast as possible. I knew, however, that as soon as I left the building, the key lessons from the class would be a distant memory. To counter my lapsed brain, I made it a point to sit down in a break area near our classroom, after each class, and create a series of notecards highlighting the key lessons the teacher discussed. Right after class, it was easy to remember the key lessons because they were still fresh in my mind. My class-to-notecard strategy only took me 15 minutes after class, but the extra effort upfront really paid off when it came time to prepare for a test. While the other students were scrambling to remember lessons from weeks ago, I got to sit back and casually flip through my notes, with an end result of acing the test.

– Tom

"I'VE ALWAYS CONSIDERED MYSELF TO BE JUST AVERAGE TALENT AND WHAT I HAVE IS A RIDICULOUS INSANE OBSESSIVENESS FOR PRACTICE AND PREPARATION."

- Will Smith

One study found that more than 80% of surveyed students admit that their use of smartphones, tablets and laptops can interfere with their learning. More than a fourth say their grades suffer as a result.[20]

THE BREAKDOWN

There are so many distractions in college: movie nights, dating, parties, family responsibilities, and we haven't even mentioned classes yet. There are, however, some learning hacks to help you excel academically in less time and with less effort.

For example, simply ask your professors, "What part of today's lecture is going to be on the exam?" It's never too early to start thinking about test preparation. By compiling notes from each lecture about what will be on the test, you will have a great collection of things to study.

Do you get distracted by regular social media notifications? There are apps that block access to a site for any time frame you set, like while you are in class.

Think of the classes you take. Do the instructors post their presentation slides ahead of time? Try printing them out before you leave for class. Don't spend the entire time writing down everything the instructor says when you can add your own notes to the slides instead. This will allow you to interact with the material, increasing your chances of retaining the information.

Pay more attention to your current class habits so you can get ahead of any bad ones that may creep up over the course of the semester. Start strong, end strong!

Let's test your memory. Think about your last class and try to remember the three most important lessons.

1: ....

2: ....

3: ....

Go back to your notes. How right were you?

1   2   3   4   5   6   7   8   9   10

Totally wrong   ———————————————   Spot on

Tip #21

F(UN-STUCK)

Clue: "Aha!" Sixteen letters. I know there is a P and an E in there somewhere. And...that's all I know. Can you guess the word? I am skipping over it for now because without more letters, who could get that answer?

I love to do crosswords. I have several crossword books, I find them in newspapers and magazines, and I even have an app on my phone that gives me several daily puzzles. It's my favorite way to train my brain for awesomeness so I stay sharp. Very often, though, I get stuck. I search and search the list of clues, but I can't think of an answer for anything. Eventually, I put it down and walk away. The next day, I come back to it and, like magic, I figure out one answer which gives me more letters and then bam, I am on a roll! While I am away from the puzzle, I often think about the clues I am stuck on, knowing that my brain is doing the work it needs to do while my prefrontal cortex is otherwise engaged. I know that if I kept sitting with that one puzzle, I wouldn't be doing my brain any favors.

Oh, and that crossword answer? The phrase "Just as I suspected" fit perfectly. I am not sure how I pulled that out of thin air, but I guess a good night's sleep helped.

- Sabina

 A study from the University of California, Santa Barbara revealed the benefits of daydreaming. Students allowed to daydream on breaks from a task came up with 41% more creative solutions than other students.[21]

THEBREAKDOWN

Staring at a problem won't crack it. The longer you look at something without gaining a new perspective, the worse you're stuck.

Next time you're stuck, confused, overwhelmed, or anything else un-fun, force yourself to get up, and do something else for a little while. This is called "getting funstuck." Grab some tea or coffee and sip it while watching a guilty pleasure TV show, or skimming through a magazine. Take a walk, take a shower, work out, take a nap, or simply focus your attention on another project you have on your list. The key here is to trust your brain to figure out the solution to your conundrum. Sometimes, a change of scenery or quick activity revitalizes the part of your brain that needed a break. Then, suddenly, a solution will come your way. And if not, at least you will have a clearer mind to get things done.

> "We cannot solve our problems with the same thinking we used when we created them."
>
> - Albert Einstein

1. Think about the last time you were stuck. What was the situation? What did you do to help yourself get un-stuck?

2. Circle which of these things you would do/have done to get f(un-stuck):

Exercise   Cup of tea/coffee

Socialize with a   Switch to
friend/ask for advice   another task

Take a shower   Read a book

Have a   Take a nap
healthy snack

Play 30 minutes   Watch a 30
of video games   minute show

GO FORTH AND BE AWESOME!

Opening up my "college memory" box over a holiday trip back home was like a walk down memory lane. I pulled out an old newspaper clipping where I was asked during an interview what I wanted to do for a living. In an effort to sound profound, I responded with, "Innovative Entrepreneur." At the time it sounded so right, but in hindsight, it sounds ridiculous. From the box, I also pulled out a pile of photos of various campus events where we all looked so young and carefree.

The thing about the good old days is that we often don't realize they are the good old days until they are gone. Upon reflection, that's how I feel about my college career. College was a lot of work and I'm happy to have graduated, but it's a period of my life filled with stories that I'll be reflecting on decades from now. It's a period of my life that will never happen again.

Despite the fact that you are only just starting your college career, and it might be hard to think about it now, graduation will show up faster than you'll realize. If we could slip in one last super secret tip to close out this book, it would be... Enjoy the ride.

You'll blink and the next thing you know you'll be getting fitted for your cap and gown. Don't let the time go by blindly. Soak up each moment. Celebrate each experience. Connect with each new friend. College is a unique opportunity that not everyone gets to experience. Instead of taking it for granted, use the time to discover and question all the wonderful things about yourself and life. College, done right, is a gift that will continue to pay dividends. Your journey starts now as you transform from a **First Year Student to a First Year Success!**

— Tom

ACKNOWLEDGEMENTS

Growing up, my idea of a published book meant that you had to disappear into a cabin in the woods for a year with a typewriter, coffee, and a dream. Now that I have a team of amazing people around me, I see book writing and publishing not as a solo sport, but rather a team effort. Each page of the book you are holding was put together by a team of talented people. It would be hard for me to tell you who wrote which parts of the book because each section involved the whole team imagining, crafting, and ultimately polishing the book to the final product that it is now. To that end, there are some people on the team that deserve special recognition for their part.

Sabina Colleran started working with me when she was fresh out of college. Beyond her contribution to the chapters, she's been a great project manager to keep everyone on track...especially me. She also used her marketing hat multiple times to define where and how to get this book out to the world with the biggest impact possible.

Melissa Ruiz brought her work experience in higher education to the table during the writing process. She was able to fill in gaps of knowledge with researched data. She also brought laughter, smiles, and hope to every editing session, which was greatly needed during parts of this process.

Between Sabina, Melissa, and I, we burned through countless dry erase markers as we locked ourselves in a conference room to make our vision for this book a reality. Through the laughing, debating, and head scratching, it slowly took shape.

Jay Chauhan was a wizard behind the scenes to help format the book. Dakota Bocan was an intern for us during the writing process, and her contributions went above and beyond the role of an intern. Lia Rothschild is a master designer and every bit of fun art you see sprinkled throughout this book is her handiwork. She also put up with our endless stream of updates and edits to each page. #SorryLia

Beyond the book writing team, I have to give a huge acknowledgement to my parents. Maryann Krieglstein (my mom) showed me that one dedicated person can make a big positive impact on the world, while Werner Krieglstein (my dad) inspired me to write as I watched him go through the process of publishing several books of his own.

Lastly, thank you to Chuck Steele and the Student Life staff at College of Dupage for seeing in me something I didn't even see in myself.

— Tom

REFERENCES

[1] Laura M. Stack, MBA, CSP, is "The Productivity PRO,"® helping people leave the office earlier, with less stress, and more to show for it. She presents keynotes and seminars on time management, information overload, and personal productivity. Contact her at 303-471-7401 or visit her website at http://www.TheProductivityPro.com.

[2] Nielsen, S., & Popkin, B. (2004). Changes in beverage intake between 1977 and 2001. *American Journal of Preventive Medicine*, 27(3), 205-210. doi: 10.1016/j.amepre.2004.05.005

[3] Dutton, J. (2012). *Make Your Bed, Change Your Life. Psychology Today*. 1991-2016 Sussex Publishers, LLC. HealthProfs.com. 2002-2016 Sussex Directories, Inc

[4] Krieglstein, Tom (professional poll to Dance Floor Theory page, February 9, 2016) asked respondents to choose which types of shoes are important for every college student to own. https://www.facebook.com/groups/dancefloortheory/permalink/9823993185 19488/?qa_ref=qd

[5] Hoyt, Elizabeth. (2013). *How Students Spend and Save*. Student News. http://www.fastweb.com/student-life/articles/how-students-spend-and-save

[6] Mattern, K., Wyatt, J.N.. (2009) Student Choice of College: How Far Do Students Go for an Education? *Journal of College Admission*, v203 p18-29 Spr 2009. http://eric.ed.gov/?id=EJ838811

[7] Hedges, K. (2015). *The Do Over: How to Correct a Bad First Impression*. Forbes.http://www.forbes.com/sites/work-in-progress/2015/02/10/the-do-over how-to-correct-a-bad-first-impression/#405debf123cc

[8] Cuseo, J. & Thompson, A. (2015). *Humanity, Diversity & The Liberal Arts: The Foundation of a College Education* (2nd ed.). Dubuque, IA: Kendall Hunt. Excerpts taken by Aaron Thompson, PhD, Eastern Kentucky University. https://webcache.googleusercontent.com/search?q=cache:G9eexmBLupMJ:htt ps://www.researchgate.net/profile/Joe_Cuseo/publication/282709430_How_Di versity_Magnifies_the_Power_of_a_College_Education/links/5619b1e808aea8(3672033c7+&cd=1&hl=en&ct=clnk&gl=us

[9]   McGonigal, Jane. (2015). *SuperBetter: A Revolutionary Approach Approach to Getting Stronger, Happier, Braver, and More Resilient.* Penguin Press. 2015. Online Forum. Superbetter, LLC. https://forums.superbetter.com/showthread.php?7-The-Basic-Science-Allies

[10]   Cross, P. K. (1998, July-August). Why learning communities? Why now? *About Campus*, pp. 4-11.

[11]   Astin, A. (1993). *What Matters in College: Four Critical Years Revisited.* Jossey-Bass Publishers, 1993 Review by David A. McKelfresh. https://www.researchgate.net/profile/Alexander_Astin/publication/242362064_What_Matters_in_College_Four_Critical_Years_Revisited/links/00b7d52d094be57582000000.pdf

[12]   Cucciara, S. (2015). *Co-Curricular Participation Drives Adult Student Excellence.* Written by Stephen Cucciara, Assistant Director of the Office of Student Activities, University of Colorado at Colorado Springs. The Evolllution: A Destiny Solutions illumination. http://evolllution.com/opinions/co-curricular-participation-drives-adult-student-excellence/

[13]   The Value of Extra-Curricular Activities Infographic. (2014). E-Learning Industry, LLC. http://elearninginfographics.com/value-extracurricular-activities-infographic/

[14]   National Institute of Mental Health. Research Date: April 27, 2015. Statistics Brain. Retreived from http://www.statisticbrain.com/fear-phobia-statistics/

[15]   U.S. Bureau of Labor Statistics. *Volunteering in the United States,* 2015. Division of Labor Force Statistics. February 25, 2016. http://www.bls.gov/news.release/volun.nr0.htm

[16]   National Association of Colleges and Associations. *Job Outlook 2016: Attributes Employers Want to See on New College Graduates' Resumes.* Spotlight for Career Services Professionals. November 18, 2015. http://www.naceweb.org/s11182015/employers-look-for-in-new-hires.aspx

[17]   Andrade, J., (2009). What Does Doodling Do? *Applied Cognitive Psychology.* Published online in Wiley InterScience (www.interscience.wiley.com) DOI: 10.1002/acp.1561. http://www.comp.dit.ie/dgordon/Courses/PSIC/doodling.pdf

[18]   Rennels, M. R., & Chaudhari, R. B. (1988). *Eye-contact and grade distribution.* Perceptual and Motor Skills, 67 (October), 627-632.

[19]   Kane, B. (2015). *Why Single-Tasking Is Your Greatest Competitive Advantage (Plus 19 Ways To Actually Do It)*. Todoist Blog. https://blog.todoist.com/2015/09/01/why-single-tasking-is-your-greatest-competitive-advantage-plus-19-ways-to-actually-do-it/.

[20]   McCoy, Bernard R., (2013). Digital Distractions in the Classroom: Student Classroom Use of Digital Devices for Non-Class Related Purposes. *Journal of Media Education*. Volume 4, Number 4. October 2013. http://en.calameo.com/read/000091789af53ca4e647f

[21]   Baird, B., Smallwood, J., Mrazek, M., Kam, J., Franklin, M., Schooler, J.. (2012). Inspired by Distraction: Mind Wandering Facilitates Creative Incubation. Association for Psychological Science. *Psychological Science OnlineFirst*, published on August 31, 2012 as doi:10.1177/0956797612446024. http://www.centenary.edu/attachments/psychology/journal/archive/2013sept journalclub.pdf

ABOUT TOM KRIEGLSTEIN

On December 5th 1980, Tom was born on a farm in Michigan where he spent the first nine years of his life. In 1999, Tom graduated high school with a stellar "C" grade point average, which led him to getting rejected from almost every college he applied. In the end, Tom enrolled at a local community college named College of DuPage. While in college, Tom discovered himself and his passion for life by getting involved in his school's co-curricular activities. It was from Tom's co-curricular activities that he grew his initial interest in Student Affairs, Student Leadership, and community engagement.

During Tom's time at College of DuPage, he was honored as a Phi Theta Kappa All-USA Academic First Team Member, Illinois Centennial Scholar, and Outstanding Graduate.

In 2001, Tom entered his final two years of college at Aurora University where he graduated top of his class in Business Management.

After a few false starts into becoming a full time professional speaker, Tom partnered with Kevin Prentiss, during their time working at Quantum Learning Network, to launch Swift Kick in 2004 and their award winning student leadership program, Dance Floor Theory. Through Tom's work in higher education, he also created The Student Affairs Collective and the NYEdTech Meetup.

On a personal note, Tom lives in New York City, is an avid runner, was named after a cat, and loves peanut butter.

Tom in College

Tom@SwiftKickHQ.com
Facebook: /TomKrieglstein
Twitter: @TomKrieglstein
Instagram: @TomKrieglstein
LinkedIn: /TomKrieglstein

Tom Now

ABOUT MELISSA RUIZ

Melissa came into this world, arm first, either raising her hand or working on her pageant wave- both would be important over the course of her life. She shares her birthday (June 27) with her awesome older brother, Michael. She attended private, Catholic school from Kindergarten through 12th grade, while residing in West Deptford, New Jersey. She excelled in the classroom (hand-raising) and preferred her dance classes and reading books to playing with dolls. At age 11, Melissa began competing in pageants (pageant waving) and had the honor to represent her town and county in several titles, using the monetary awards for winning to start a small college fund. Along with a promise from her mother to pay for Melissa's education (Thanks Mom!), she graduated from Rutgers University- Douglass College with a Bachelor of Art degree in Psychology. While attending college, she continued to compete in pageants, earning more than $5,000 in scholarships.

In her second year at Rutgers, Melissa was hired as a Summer Conference Assistant for Conference Services and Peer Academic Leader in the Residence Life department; in her third year, she was a Resident Assistant and on the Executive Board of Annual Women's Weekend, an organization on campus. Once again, academics were a strength, allowing her to complete her undergraduate degree in 3 years. She went on to obtain her Master of Social Work degree at the age of 22, while working as a hall director, continuing to serve the freshman population on the Douglass Campus.

Since then, she has worked in several areas of student affairs, including student leadership and engagement, orientation and academic advising. Her work in higher education led her to the Swift Kick team, allowing her to impact students' lives on a larger scale.

She would like to extend thanks to the following: Tom and Sabina, for accepting her weirdness with open arms. To her friends and family, for their support and encouragement; to the Miss America Organization, scholarship, style, service and success will always be with her.

Melissa in College

Melissa Now

Melissa@SwiftKickHQ.com

Facebook: /Melissa.Angela.Ruiz

Twitter: @Melissa_A_Ruiz

Instagram: @melissa.a.ruiz

ABOUT SABINA COLLERAN

Sabina graduated from Fordham University in 2013, with a degree in psychology and a minor in business administration. She was an active participant and board member of FUPAC (the Filipino club on campus) for four years and considers it to be her family. She also served as an Orientation Leader. Although she commuted back and forth to campus, she didn't let that stop her from making the most of the college experience. At the time of writing, she served on the Fordham Young Alumni Committee where she continued to celebrate her love of all things Fordham.

Sabina works as the Community Manager for Swift Kick, which began as her first job out of college. In the office, she is part time writer, part time travel booker, part time manager, and part time marketing and social media ninja. She often holds the office "Weird Card" (that's a real thing) and makes as many jokes as she can during meetings.

Outside of work, Sabina reads all the books, writes poetry, obsessively does crosswords, and crafts. She has successfully transitioned from being called "mom" by everyone, to being a total grandma. Her life goal is to be a perpetual ball of sunshine.

In the making of this book, she would like to thank the following:
Tom and Melissa: For being amazing co-workers, mentors, and friends. The laughs and camaraderie make all the hard work feel like no work at all.

Mom, Dad, Christian, and Martine: For being a supportive and loving family who is as excited as she is that she co-wrote a book.

Kieran: For being a supportive, fantastic husband who listens to her incessant chatter about college and her awesome job, and celebrates with her

Fordham University: For giving her an experience she was able to draw so much inspiration from, especially when writing this book. She would not be the person she is today without those precious four years.

God: For always putting her in the right place at the right time, as the person she is. #AMDG

Sabina in College

Sabina Now

Sabina@SwiftKickHQ.com

Twitter: @SabinaDeelight

Instagram: @SabinaDeelight

ABOUT

Six-Time Campus Speakers of the Year, and Performer of the Year, Swift Kick, has trained over 550,000 campus leaders on how to create a culture of engagement, from orientation to graduation, where everyone feels welcomed, connected and engaged. Their main leadership program, "Dance Floor Theory Leadership Training" helps campus leaders see and understand the challenges and opportunities of engagement on their campus in a new way. For more information on Swift Kick and their trainings, or to bring a program to your campus, visit www.swiftkickhq.com.

Facebook: /SwiftKickHQ

Twitter: @SwiftKickHQ

Instagram: @SwiftKickHQ

NOTES

NOTES

NOTES

37017910R00060

Made in the USA
San Bernardino, CA
26 May 2019